"In this world of swagger, Jes
serve—him, one another, an
beautifully as we come togethe
ant heart. Thank you, Steve, fo. ......g .....s ᴜᴜᴜᴋ and inspiring all
of us to give our hearts away!"

RAY ORTLUND, Renewal Ministries, Nashville, TN;
Author, *You're Not Crazy*

"Drawing on 20 years of church leadership experience, Steve teach-
es us how and why we should serve in the church, motivates us
to follow the example of Jesus from a heart of love for him, and
encourages us to persevere in service. Study questions make this
short book ideal to read and discuss in small groups. Every church
will be strengthened if they read this stirring challenge."

JOHN STEVENS, National Director, FIEC, UK

"One of the wonderful privileges of belonging to God's family is
that we get to serve him by serving one another. But it doesn't
always feel like a privilege. It's easy to lose our sense of purpose
and motivation, and become weary and discouraged. In this de-
lightful book, Steve reminds us of the 'who' and 'why' of our serving. This book left me humbled by my Saviour's example, grateful
for opportunities to reflect his servant heart and determined to
joyfully follow his example."

CAROLYN LACEY, Author, *Say the Right Thing*
and *(Extra)Ordinary Hospitality*

"In this warm, pastoral book, Steve Robinson provides us with a
resource that is biblically rich and deeply relatable for why serving
one another is vital to being a healthy church. Read it to remember
how Jesus has meaningfully included us in his work. But even
more than that, read it to remember the glory and beauty and
example of the God whom we are serving."

ADAM RAMSEY, Lead Pastor, Liberti Church, Gold Coast,
Australia; Director, Acts29 Asia Pacific; Author, *Truth on Fire*

"This little book is simple, clear, warm and practical. It's definitely
worth a few pounds of anybody's money."

MEZ McCONNELL, Director, 20Schemes,
Author, *The Least, the Last and the Lost*

"Oftentimes, the idea of serving in our local churches comes from a posture of obligation rather than a response to the gospel. This book makes a compelling argument for a gospel-driven heart of serving others with compassion in Jesus' name. Inspiring, impassioned and thoughtful, *Serve* will provoke discussions and prompt change, bringing about gospel-centered results for many years."

DOUG LOGAN, JR., President, Grimké Seminary and College;
Author, *On the Block*

"Wise, clear and fortifying, here is a book that proves we can serve Christ and his church with love and joy even through the tough times. Steve Robinson shows how the gospel enables us to serve wholeheartedly, whatever our situation, even in our weaknesses and failures. Read and be encouraged!"

MICHAEL REEVES, President, Union School of Theology;
Author, *Rejoice and Tremble*

"Consumerism used to be one vice among many—yet today it's one of the most widely-agreed-upon foundations for the good life. We desperately need a more compelling vision. With pastoral warmth and biblical wisdom, Steve Robinson calls us back to the beauty of being conformed into the image of the one who came not to be served but to serve. I'm confident this book will help equip many to give their lives away for the glory of God and the good of others."

JOSH KOURI, Lead Pastor, Frontline Church, Oklahoma City, OK

"I can't think of anyone better suited to write a book on this subject! I have had the privilege of watching this brother lovingly serve his family and his church through some of the toughest seasons imaginable and he has done so humbly, faithfully and in ways that modelled dependence on and devotion to Jesus. I pray that what's written in these pages will encourage and inspire you to serve the Son of Man who didn't come to be served but to serve and give his life as a ransom for you."

DAI HANKEY, Church planter; Founder, Red Community;
Author, *Hopeward*

serve

STEVE ROBINSON

Serve
Loving Your Church with Your Heart, Time and Gifts
© 2023 Steve Robinson

Published by:
The Good Book Company

thegoodbook.com | thegoodbook.co.uk
thegoodbook.com.au | thegoodbook.co.nz | thegoodbook.co.in

Original series cover design by Faceout Studio | Art direction and design by André Parker

ISBN: 9781784989163 | JOB-007283-1 | Printed in Turkey

To my wife, Siân –

I am so thankful that the Lord gave me you to serve alongside. You are a blessing to many. Love you.

To my children, Ella, Lilly, Elijah and Joshua –

I pray you will know the joy of serving Jesus and his church. Love you.

CONTENTS

FOREWORD

BY BRIAN HOWARD

Throughout the centuries, countless Christians have heeded the call to serve, driven by their faith and the teachings of Christ. Their stories of devotion and sacrifice are woven into the tapestry of our history, reminding us of the transformative power of service and inspiring us to follow in their footsteps. Christians have manifested service by feeding the hungry, clothing the naked, healing the sick and providing shelter to the homeless. They have fought for justice, advocated for the marginalized, and stood as voices of compassion in the face of adversity. They have served God, their families, communities, and local churches. Many Christians who have long since gone to be with Jesus are known by us today because of their lives of service.

One record of this servant-hearted approach to life is found on a tombstone in North Hampton, Massachusetts, that reads:

Sacred to the memory of the Rev. David Brainerd. A faithful and laborious Missionary to the Stockbridge,

Delaware, and Susquehanna Tribes of Indians, who died in this town. Oct. 10, 1747.

David Brainerd was often sick, struggled with depression, and only lived to be 29 years old. But because he was willing to use what he had to serve God, there are several hundred Native Americans who owe their everlasting life to his ministry.

In today's world, where self-interest often dominates, the concept of service is not on the societal intuitive front-burner in any way. But serving does remain the essence of the Christian life. Through living a life of Christ-like service, we have the opportunity to be used by God to transform those around us as they encounter a countercultural way of living. Christians who view life through the lens of service have the opportunity to reshape our communities and impact the lives of those around us in profound ways.

Over my 35 years of adulthood and 33 years of ministry, I have endeavored to serve as a way of life. This commitment for me seems to be essential for living in a gospel-centered way. I was motivated first by understanding that Jesus had come not to be served but to serve (Mark 10:45). I read of the apostle Paul describing himself as a servant (Romans 1:1). I found Epaphroditus in Philippians 2 and noticed that Paul said he deserved to be honored simply for his mundane acts of service. And then I learned about serving from watching my dad put our family first and being mentored by older leaders who served well.

As a college student, I began to look for opportunities to serve. I joined a church-planting team. I served in a local church by leading worship and teaching the Bible to a few teenagers. After college, I married and began a 30-year-long journey of serving my wife. Over these years, we raised four (now adult) children. Throughout my time in vocational ministry, I have looked to serve God, the local church and my neighbors. My aim has always been to see myself as a servant. I do not have a perfect record of doing so, but I have sought to remain true to this commitment.

So it is with great pleasure that I introduce this excellent book by Steve Robinson, which explores the depth and beauty of Christians serving as a way of life. I have known Steve for many years, and he has devoted his life to gospel-centered service to God, his family, his community and his church. Within the pages of this profoundly helpful work, you will embark on a journey that delves into the beauty and depth of serving as a way of life. Steve examines the biblical teaching that underpins the dedication to serving as a way of life. And he explores the deep-rooted connection between Christian faith and service, illuminating the theological foundations that have propelled individuals and communities to follow in the footsteps of Jesus.

Christians are called to bring hope, love and compassion to those around us. At its core, service is an expression of love—of God and of those around us. It is a selfless act that transcends personal gain and embraces the example of Jesus himself. Ultimately, this book serves as a rallying call to all Christians, inviting us all to embrace serving as a way of life. It challenges us to examine our priorities, question our motivations and live our lives as an embodiment of Christ's teachings. As you read this excellent book, may you be inspired, encouraged and empowered to live a life of service, infused with the love and compassion that lies at the heart of Christianity.

Brian Howard
President, Acts29

1. WHO DO WE SERVE?

My wife and I are two of the tens of millions of people who became hooked on the TV series *Downton Abbey*. We were fascinated by the lives of the aristocratic Crawley family and their domestic servants on their fictional country estate in early 20th-century Britain. We enjoyed it so much that we even became members of the National Trust.

For a working-class lad born into a two-up-two-down house in a deprived area of Liverpool in the 1970s, my experience (like most people's) is a million miles away from the aristocratic families who used to reside in these grand mansions. But I confess that I have said to my wife, Siân, on several—ok, on many—occasions that I think I could *just about* have handled that life. I especially think this on day trips to country houses as we pass through grand studies, enormous living rooms and vast grounds.

The other area of these households that fascinates me is what was known as the "downstairs". The life of these old aristocratic homes was kept going by the service of those who lived and worked downstairs—the butlers, footmen, lady's maids, cooks and kitchen hands. These roles were taken up by local people who lived within the house and served the families that employed them. It wasn't viewed as casual employment but as a dedication of their lives to service and, hopefully, if the family were kind, a dedication to that particular family. To do the best job, these staff had to know exactly who they were serving—by learning the ins and outs of the master's and mistress's habits, likes, dislikes and temperaments. They also needed to serve each other through their different roles downstairs—the cook still needed to prepare staff meals and the maids still needed to lay the fires for the staff. And outside of the household, they were fully aware that they represented that family to the surrounding towns and villages that relied on the success of the House. They were serving their master, each other and the local community.

Like the servants in these grand houses, as Christians we are called to serve. One way of describing what happens when someone becomes a Christian is to say that they have "turned to God from idols to serve the living and true God, and to wait for his Son from heaven" (1 Thessalonians 1:9-10). The word "servant" doesn't *fully* describe who we are as Christians, but it is *part* of who we are as Christians. And, just as in those country houses, when it comes to our service, who we are serving matters more than what we are doing in our serving. In other words, we need to know first and foremost exactly who it is we are serving. Really understanding this will be the foundation that determines why and how we serve, and will give purpose and meaning to our lives.

WE SERVE GOD

Genesis 1 declares that we have been made in the image of God. God's plan and desire in his design was for humanity to display his image here on earth. As people walked, worked, played, interacted, engaged in relationships, had children (multiplying more image-bearers) and created culture, his glory would increase. God gave humans everything we needed to represent and serve him fully. We were to live a life of joyful service with our Master walking beside us. Not with him living upstairs and us living downstairs but with God's presence right in our midst, with him being glorified in our service.

But the desire to be served and the desire for self-glory captured the affections of the first humans. As a result of their disobedience to God's word, sin entered the world, and the human image of God was distorted. Our intentions became selfish, and we lost sight of the God whom the first humans had joyfully served, and we became afraid of him. Humanity was cast out of his life-giving presence, with death becoming our ultimate destiny—this is the tragedy recounted in Genesis 3. In the book of Romans, Paul sums it up like this:

"They [humans] exchanged the truth about God for a
lie and worshipped and served the creature rather than
the Creator, who is blessed for ever!" (Romans 1:25)

People ended up serving themselves rather than God and others. They sought to sit in the Master's place. And as generations came and went, one thing remained the same: the determination of humans to put themselves first and expect the world to revolve around them.

But God wasn't done with humanity. The book of Exodus is the story of God freeing, forming and communing with the people he had promised to restore to relationship with himself but who had been in slavery for 400 years under the oppressive regime of the Egyptians. One of these Hebrews, Moses, was chosen by God to lead his people out of slavery and into the promised land. He famously brought the order from God to Pharaoh to "let my people go", but the second part of God's demand is often forgotten:

"Then the LORD said to Moses, 'Go in to Pharaoh and
say to him, "Thus says the LORD, 'Let my people go,
that they may serve me.'"'" (Exodus 8:1)

God's command to let his people go was for the purpose of *serving him*. There was a plan for and a purpose to their freedom. God was redeeming his image-bearers so they could serve him and display his glory. He gave them hope for the future and an opportunity to serve their Creator freely, rather than a life of slavery to "created things". The exodus story foreshadows the redemption that Christians have in Jesus. We have been saved, freed and forgiven, thanks to the grace and mercy of God and the resurrection of Jesus Christ from the dead. We can now know the one whom we have been created to serve; we can walk with him and enjoy him.

In his letter to the church in Ephesus, Paul reminds the believers that they were once dead in sin but now are alive in Christ, all because of God's grace and mercy and nothing to do with their own efforts. We are saved—but what next?

> *"For we are his workmanship, created in Christ Jesus for good works, which God prepared beforehand, that we should walk in them." (Ephesians 2:10)*

In other words, we have been saved and restored for good works of service that display his glory to the world. And it's not a life of drudgery that is in store for us— our Master has personally prepared good works for us to do. We have been saved to serve him, giving us a joyful purpose to our lives.

Who do we serve? We serve a loving Creator, who is not upstairs waiting for our service but rather is in us and with us, enabling us to serve him for his glory. We serve God.

WE SERVE THE CHURCH

I love football (or soccer, if you're in North America—but in this book, we'll call it football). I love playing it (well,

I used to), I love coaching it and I love watching it. The past few years have been good to me because I've enjoyed my team, Liverpool Football Club, being one of the best in the world. There are many reasons why Liverpool have reached the pinnacle of world football—we have great players, great fans and great coaches. But I think the key element for the club's success is one Jurgen Norbert Klopp—a former average second-tier German footballer who has become widely regarded as one of the greatest managers on the planet.

The story goes that on his first day at the club, he gathered the team in the canteen along with all the support staff: cleaners, administration assistants, groundsmen and so on. Then he asked the superstar players if they knew the names of those employees. The response was embarrassing... Klopp said that that needed to change; he told the players that without these staff serving them, success on the pitch would never happen. Each of the support staff also wore the team badge on their uniforms and were a vital part of the Liverpool FC family and the success of the club. From that moment, the players would eat with support staff and get to know them, and everyone would serve each other because, he said, "We are Liverpool, and this means more".

God hasn't called a few select superstars to be served by a mass of believers that no one really knows. He has saved a people whose distinctive quality is to be their love for each other. In Eden (Genesis 1 – 3), Adam was unable to truly reflect the glory and image of God on his own, so Eve was created as his helper. *Together* as God's people, Adam and Eve were able to display his glory as they served each other and served him. But when they turned away from God, they turned towards serving themselves—Adam didn't love, lead and protect Eve, and Eve didn't trust the word of Adam that came from the word of God. The reflection of God's loving image was shattered, and their love for one another was marred.

Later, in Genesis 12, God promised Abraham that he would make him into a great nation that would be a blessing to the world. Through Abraham's line, God had chosen and saved a people (the Hebrews) whom he would cherish:

> *"Now therefore, if you will indeed obey my voice and keep my covenant, you shall be my treasured possession among all peoples." (Exodus 19:5)*

Through their obedience to God's word, they were to be a holy nation (v 6)—a people set apart, who functioned and engaged with each other based on an understanding of the glory and goodness of God. They were to be a kingdom of priests: devoted to the service of God and to each other, and distinct from other nations in how they lived, loved and served him and each other through following his law.

These early promises to Israel reflect the promises of God to his church today. In his letter to struggling Christians who were trying to live for Jesus in a hostile culture, Peter uses those words from Exodus 19 to remind the Christians who they are as God's people:

> *"But you are a chosen race, a royal priesthood, a holy nation, a people for his own possession, that you may proclaim the excellencies of him who called you out of darkness into his marvellous light. Once you were not a people, but now you are God's people; once you had not received mercy, but now you have received mercy."*
> *(1 Peter 2:9-10)*

Even though the world rejects them (v 2), they are to continue to love one another with a sincere brotherly love which is grounded in their knowledge of God's grace and mercy. Peter is saying that because of what Jesus achieved in dying and rising from the dead, they—and we too—are now his people living in this world, moving towards the promise of a secure inheritance. And what sets us apart as his people is the way we love each other, engage with each other and serve each other before a watching world.

There is no service to God that doesn't include service to each other as his church, whatever the circumstances. Right after Jesus had stooped to wash the dusty, dirty feet of his disciples, he gave them a new commandment:

> *"Love one another: just as I have loved you, you also are to love one another. By this all people will know*

*that you are my disciples, if you have love for one
another." (John 13:34-35)*

Jesus' actions and words combined present a picture to
us of the kind of humility and love that distinguishes us
as his followers. The Liverpool FC staff were encouraged
by Jurgen Klopp to serve each other because they all
wore the team emblem—each and every one of them
played a part in achieving the club's goals (quite literally).
In serving God, we need to know that we are to serve
each other because each of us is a part of God's treasured
possession. To put it another way, we need to remember
that God does not save us as individuals but as a people,
bringing each of us into his family. Your church are your
brothers and sisters, and you're given to each other to
serve one another, in order to serve God.

Who do we serve? We serve our brothers and sisters, the
family God has put us in. We serve the church.

WE SERVE THE WORLD

Let's recap a couple of the verses we've already looked at:

We exist...

*"that [we] may proclaim the excellencies of him who
called [us] out of darkness into his marvellous light."*
(1 Peter 2:9)

*"By this all people will know that you are my disciples, if
you have love for one another." (John 13:35)*

Who do we proclaim the excellencies of God to? We proclaim them to him, as our way of recognising his greatness, and we proclaim them to each other, as our way of encouraging our family, but we also proclaim them to the world. If we serve each other in the sacrificial way Jesus loved and served us, people will know that we are his disciples. Our service to God and each other flows out in compassion and mercy to serve a world that needs to hear and know the glory of the God who has saved us. In displaying his glory to us, God calls us to display that glory to the world, as Peter shows:

> "Keep your conduct among the Gentiles honourable, so that when they speak against you as evildoers, they may see your good deeds and glorify God on the day of visitation." (1 Peter 2:12)

As we, God's people, serve our neighbours, friends and colleagues through our honourable conduct, our kind deeds and our sharing of the gospel message, the world is blessed—even if the world doesn't see that, or even rejects and ridicules us because of it.

Who do we serve? We serve a world which desperately needs to see that there is a loving God who wants to save and restore people.

This is a book about serving. And we will be getting practical. I hope this book will leave you more equipped for serving than you were when you opened it. But before you figure out what it means to serve as a

Christian and a member of your local church, you need to know exactly who it is you are serving. You need to know who you are and what your purpose is. But it's also good to know what the one you are serving thinks of you. In Bible times, kings would keep the valued possessions that they held most dear on their person or in close quarters. You may not think you're held dear by many people or even anybody at all, but you are God's treasured possession, you are dear to him, and he chooses to display his glory through you by preparing great things for you to do in his cause—works of service that reflect and reveal his love. That is why we serve. And being excited about serving the God who loves us in this way will leave us wanting to be equipped for serving. We get to serve the greatest of all masters. We are God's people, who have the great honour and privilege of serving him, the church, and the world.

ACTION STEPS

- Why is it helpful to keep in mind a deep knowledge of who you are serving?

- How does 1 Peter 2:9-10 help you to understand both who you are and who you are to serve?

- In the moments when you are tempted to serve self, what is it about the gospel that helps you run from that to embrace the gift of serving God, the church and the world?

2. WHY DO WE SERVE?

Queen Elizabeth II, who ascended to the throne on 6th February 1952 and who reigned for 70 years till her death on 8th September 2022, was respected, loved and admired by many around the world. The news of her death was one of those moments that most of us will remember for the rest of our lives.

Of the thousands of pictures of the queen that we saw during the lead-up to her funeral, one of the most striking images for me was the last photograph taken of her, two days before she died. She was pictured fulfilling her constitutional obligation and service in welcoming and commissioning Liz Truss, the incoming prime minister of Great Britain. The Queen was clearly physically frail and weary, but with a beaming smile on her face, she stood and undertook what turned out to be her final duty as the queen of the United Kingdom and the Commonwealth. This epitomised Queen Elizabeth's attitude to her role. During the ten or so years before her death, there was much speculation and debate over whether she would abdicate the throne and hand the crown to her eldest son, Charles. But it's clear from what has been shared since her death that, as far as the queen was concerned, her role was an anointing from God for life. She had made a promise that she would fulfil this role before God and the nation, and she intended to do so, every day. Of course, she found herself in a privileged position that she had not earned or deserved—but she embraced the responsibility that came with it, giving herself to serve her people. But not just her people— she was serving her God. On the day of her coronation in 1953, before she made promises to her subjects or was anointed and crowned, she walked to the front of Westminster Abbey alone, and in silence prayed private prayers of allegiance to God. And she remained loyal to him each day of the rest of her life.

For 70 years Queen Elizabeth II knew why she was serving. In any service, it's the "why" behind what we are doing that enables us to do it. The dad who takes a job that he is totally over-qualified for—so he can be home to read the Bible with his kids each night and be available to serve in his weekly small group—knows the answer to the why question. The woman in Mozambique who walks three miles a day to collect fresh water—not just for her family but for another family in her church— knows the answer. The single mother who works three jobs while raising two kids and still makes sure they have a family Bible time most mornings knows the answer.

The young person who gives up their Friday nights to support a couple in their home group who have children with additional needs knows the answer.

The answer to why we serve God, the church and the world is... because we follow Jesus. We often over-complicate the reasons, but it's simple—our Lord and Saviour, Jesus, said, in Mark 10:45: "For even the Son of Man came not to be served but to serve, and to give his life as a ransom for many".

We are disciples of Jesus.

Jesus came to serve.

So we follow suit.

As Paul puts it:

> "Do nothing from rivalry or conceit, but in humility count others more significant than yourselves. Let each of you look not only to his own interests, but also to the interests of others. Have this mind among yourselves, which is yours in Christ Jesus, who, though he was in the form of God, did not count equality with God a thing to be grasped, but made himself nothing, taking the form of a servant, being born in the likeness of men." (Philippians 2:3-7)

WHAT MAKES THIS HARD

What complicates and distorts this simple truth is that by nature we follow our own minds rather than the mind of Christ. A lot of the time, we don't operate from a position of humility. We want, even if it's only a tiny dose, some self-satisfaction, affirmation or even glory for our service. We want to serve in ways that are comfortable and fit round our real priorities. This isn't new—this is one of humanity's inherent problems. In fact, Jesus told his disciples that he had come to serve and not to be served in response to a request made by James and John to have position and glory in his kingdom:

> "And James and John, the sons of Zebedee, came up to him and said to him, 'Teacher, we want you to do for us whatever we ask of you.' And he said to them, 'What do you want me to do for you?' And they said to him, 'Grant us to sit, one at your right hand and one at your left, in your glory.'" (Mark 10:35-36)

When the other disciples heard this they were not happy (v 41)—not because of the selfishness of the brothers' request but because they wanted those positions just as much.

For six years I worked for a well-known Christian relief and development organisation which runs the largest Christmas shoebox appeal in the world. Millions of people from the UK, USA, Canada, Germany and Australia fill paper-wrapped shoeboxes with gifts and sweets for needy children all around the world. It's an amazing project that not only blesses the millions of children who receive or who make the gifts, but also the thousands of volunteers who collect, check, and pack the shoeboxes for distribution every year. One of the joys that I had was to serve alongside many people in cold warehouses all across the UK, ensuring that the boxes were packed away safely on lorries and in containers and then shipped off to places like Liberia, Kosovo and Ukraine.

On many occasions I asked the volunteers, "Why do you do this?" and often the answer would be "For the kids". I know that most people meant it, and that was the reason why they stood in the cold for hours. But I saw several volunteers walk away from serving, even though their answer was "For the kids"—and not because there were no kids to serve but because of something else. They didn't like the warehouse; they didn't like the new volunteer team lead; they felt taken for granted—and so on. I understand that circumstances do change and sometimes it's right for people to move on, but in these cases the "why" simply wasn't enough to sustain their desire to serve through change or discomfort. Dare I say it, the real "why" wasn't the kids (or wasn't only the kids); rather, it was self.

I've been in Christian ministry for 20 years, and most of that time I have been involved or connected in some way or another to church planting. I recall being in a conference seminar which was about planting churches in deprived areas. The person leading the seminar wrote on the whiteboard, *Why do you serve where you serve?* After some discussion around tables, people shared feedback, and the most popular answer to the question was "Because we love the people".

I'll never forget the silence in the room when the person leading the seminar said, "That's not enough".

He went on to say that, yes, it is important and right that we love the people that we serve—that we have the compassion of Christ and can be moved to tears when we walk around our neighbourhood and see the pain, suffering and lostness. But what happens when you find that you don't love the people anymore? How do you respond when the people that you have poured your life into turn their back on you or, worse, turn their back on Jesus? How will you feel towards the church family when you are struggling to pay the bills or buy Christmas presents for your kids because the offering is short? What do you do when you don't love the people? You stop serving.

WE SERVE BECAUSE HE FIRST SERVED US

As Christians, the "why" of our serving can't be any less (and needn't be any more) than... Jesus—because, if it is, when the circumstances of our lives or the conditions of our service change, we will walk away—either literally or emotionally. We need to remember that the "why" behind our perseverance is something and someone that never changes.

In his letter to the church in Rome, Paul urges his brothers and sisters to give themselves as living sacrifices, in light of the mercies of God that he has so wonderfully explained for them in the first eleven chapters of his letter.

> *"I appeal to you therefore, brothers, by the mercies of God, to present your bodies as a living sacrifice, holy and acceptable to God, which is your spiritual worship. Do not be conformed to this world, but be transformed by the renewal of your mind, that by testing you may discern what is the will of God, what is good and acceptable and perfect." (Romans 12:1-2)*

According to Paul, our worship isn't just a Sunday thing or a Tuesday-evening-at-small-group thing; it's so much more than that. Believing and accepting what Jesus has done means giving our bodies and our minds—in essence, our whole lives—to God. That means giving time, money, homes, marriages, kids, possessions... giving ourselves even to the point of losing life itself.

We are to give our whole lives as *living sacrifices*.

For the early Christians, the concept of sacrifice was understood in the context of the sacrificial system that God had put in place for his people. Before the death and resurrection of Jesus, animal sacrifice was the means by which God's people could approach him, be made right with him, and petition and pray to him. The sacrificial offerings required the death of an animal which was without any blemish. The blood of that animal was poured, smeared or sprinkled onto the altar, which paid for the sins of the people and made them right before God. This sacrificial obedience was pleasing to him (see Leviticus 1 – 7). But when Paul says, "By the mercies of God... present your bodies as a living sacrifice", he's not talking about the sacrificing of animals or a literal sacrificing of self in order to be right with God. He is saying, *Consider the mercies of God, who gave his Son, Jesus Christ, to die in our place as the ultimate sacrifice, taking the punishment that we deserve, atoning for our sin, conquering the grave, making us alive in him and promising us a future glory with him. Considering all that, present your bodies as living sacrifices as an act of worship.* He's saying that to live for Jesus—to give everything you have to him and to serve him with all that you are—is the only rational response to his mercy and grace.

To put it another way, we are called to serve wholeheartedly, sacrificially, daily. It is a high and hard calling. The only thing that will see us get on with that kind of serving is an equally glorious reason. And that is what we have. You will serve like that to the extent that you consider Jesus and are awed by his love for you and service to you. Why do we serve as living sacrifices? Because we know Jesus.

HOLDING ON TO OUR "WHY"

The reason why we serve God and his church never changes. But we're quick to forget that when circumstances become uncomfortable, discouraging or overwhelming. It's easy to allow uncomfortable change or a lack of affirmation to be the reasons why we give up. These moments reveal the real "why" that we're holding onto in our service. There are times where we may be legitimately exhausted and need to scale back or take a break to find our comfort and energy in him through rest. There are times when it's legitimate to ask others in our church to help encourage us as we serve. But often, when we're disgruntled and tired and feeling like giving up, what we need is to remind ourselves of Jesus' love and find our purpose in serving him again, to keep going.

So, when you are the only person picking up the bulletins from the floor after the Sunday service or stacking chairs when everyone else has left; when you're driving home after preaching your heart out and no one has thanked you; when the young people start to say they're bored with your youth meeting; when you've spent hours making a meal for people in church and no one turns up; or when you're just tired of serving and giving and you start to ask the question: *why am I doing this?*— remember Romans 12:1. The why behind your service is God's mercy. The "why" behind your service is Jesus, who, in love for you, gave up everything for you.

THINKING IT THROUGH

In some senses, the most important part of serving is how you think about serving. As Paul tells the Romans, to live sacrificially you need to think rightly—to not be conformed to this world's way of thinking but rather to be transformed by the renewal of your mind (v 2). Before we received God's mercy, we were all conformed to this world's way of thinking and living. We dishonoured our bodies (Romans 1:24); we served what was created rather than the Creator (v 25); we suppressed the truth (v 18); and we arrogantly decided that we were wise (v 22). If we do not ask and allow God to continually transform our minds, we can slip back into thinking like this again— even in our Christian service. It becomes about us and about wanting people to affirm or even worship us. We serve to be noticed by others rather than by God. We serve for the thank-you we get from the pastor or to be liked by the youth group, and if we get that, then it is all worth it. But then, sooner or later, we will walk away because the lack of thanks is damaging our self-esteem.

Later in Romans 12, Paul tells us that we should outdo each other in showing honour (v 10). I know it's discouraging when we are not honoured, but honouring others is part of our service to him and the church, as we'll see in a later chapter. When we make being honoured a condition of our service, it clouds the reason why we serve. Our culture often says, "Unless I'm appreciated or satisfied, I'm not going to do it"—but this stands right in the face of Paul's appeal for sacrifice. He tells us not to "be conformed" to this way of thinking. We have been given the mind of Jesus (1 Corinthians 1:16). We are able to think as he does and honour others as he does. It does remain a struggle to do this because our sinful nature wants to suppress this truth and wants what is created (that is, ourselves) to be glorified more than him. By nature, we want recognition, we want to be honoured and we want to be praised. We want to be served rather than serve. So we need to ask his Spirit to enable us to think like Jesus, who, for the joy set before him, endured the cross, walking headlong into shame and pain in obedience to his Father, to serve us and to save us (Hebrews 12:2).

Two questions have been ringing through my head while I've been writing this chapter: *Do I present my body as a living sacrifice? Do I give everything or do I just give a section of my life?* These are questions I can't seem to shake.

I recall hearing stories of missionaries a century or two ago travelling from the UK to places like India, China and beyond, who would ship their belongings in coffin-shaped boxes because leaving home to serve God in proclaiming the gospel almost certainly meant not coming back. It meant death in the field of service. Do I have the same attitude to serving God? Do you? I want to serve in a way that displays genuine gospel love to my brothers and sisters at church, and I want to continue serving when it's inconvenient for me or when the people in my community are hard to love (or, at least, I want to want to serve like that). And I will only do that—and you will only do that—if the answer to why we are doing it is Jesus. The way we serve will be an overflow of our hearts. If our hearts have been captured by the mercies of God in Jesus, then we will want to serve even when things don't go the way we want them to or prove to be harder than we'd expected them to be. This reason to serve sustains us when we are tired and everything in us wants to give up. Why do we serve? Because of Jesus. And he's enough.

ACTION STEPS

- How does knowing the mercy of God motivate your service?

- What are the tipping points that cause you to embrace the world's way of thinking when serving is tough?

- What is it about how Jesus served on earth and serves us now that encourages you in your service?

- Pray that your heart is captured by the mercies of God and that you are able, with his strength, to present your whole life sacrificially for his service.

3. GOOD AND FAITHFUL SERVANT

When I die, I want to hear God say to me, "Well done, good and faithful servant" (Matthew 25:23, NIV). Can you imagine what that moment will be like? For the Creator to look at you and greet you as a son or daughter and then praise your service of him?

What will it take for us to hear him say that? What is faithful service? That's the subject of this chapter. But here's a summary: it will require us to sustain our service and for it to be an imitation of the way Jesus served.

SUSTAINING IS HARDER THAN STARTING

Becoming a police officer was a dream come true for me. It was what I wanted to be when I grew up (second only to becoming a footballer in the English Premier League), and at 19 years of age, I became one of the youngest officers in the Merseyside Police. I took an oath at a swearing-in ceremony, promising that I would serve the queen, country and community in upholding the law.

Being the youngest police officer in my city meant that I was given the jobs that no one else wanted to do, like making the tea for other officers or doing traffic duty at school home time—but I didn't care. I was happy to help, and I was living my boyhood dream of wearing that police uniform. Older officers, or at least those who had been in the job more than five minutes longer than me, said things like "I remember when I was like you". Most of them were good at their jobs, but their enthusiasm levels were very different to mine. Their main driver was retirement (police officers in the UK get a great retirement package), and everything was geared towards the day when they would finish.

After a couple of years, I found myself talking about how great retirement was going to be too. I was only 21 years old! For these officers, and increasingly for me, the motivation and reason to serve in the police had shifted. The joy and privilege of doing that job had gone. Many of us seemed just to be going through the motions.

To an extent, this is natural in any job; the Bible does tell us that because of sin, work is toil, even for the most enthusiastic and motivated of people. Whether you're a Christian or not, the joy of a new job fades, and it easily becomes the pay cheque, the benefits, the status or the thought of retirement that becomes the motivating and sustaining factor for continued work.

The fulfilment of my dream launched my career as a cop with great joy, but the initial motivation was never going to be enough to sustain that joy for a lifetime's service. Sustaining is harder than starting.

It's the same in the Christian life.

THE START

What more reason and motivation do you need to give your life in service to God? He has saved you, forgiven you and made you his child—it's a no-brainer!

This is a paraphrase of something my next-door neighbour Freddie said in conversation with me.

Freddie became a Christian about four years ago. He is from a completely non-Christian, unchurched background. He had no concept of what it meant to live as a follower of Jesus or function as a church member. In fact, Freddie became a believer before he had even set foot in a church. I remember him sitting at the kitchen table in our house and saying, "If there is anything I can do for anyone in the church, please let me know. I can't do much, but I can take people for coffee to encourage them, or I could clean the church." Freddie hadn't met anyone from church apart from me and my family, but he had an overwhelming desire to serve God and his people. The starting point was his newfound love for Jesus Christ.

In Romans 12:1, as we've seen, Paul calls this "spiritual worship". The word "spiritual" in the original Greek language means something more like "rational" or "reasonable". It has the sense of being true to nature. So Freddie's motivation to serve came from his new sense of gratitude, worth and purpose as a follower of Jesus. For all of us who have been saved by God's grace, serving means living true to our new nature as disciples. It's responding rationally to what God has done for us; it's embracing our new identity—it's a no-brainer.

Freddie's mind had been renewed (v 2). If you spoke to him, Freddie would tell you that before coming to know Jesus, Freddie was all about Freddie. But now he wanted to serve someone other than himself. He wanted to serve God and his people.

But sooner or later, Freddie's hunger to serve may well wane. It won't seem such a no-brainer. Maybe you have been a Christian long enough to look back on a time when it all seemed so obvious and straightforward. Now, though, not so much.

SUSTAINING IT

I had been in the police for a few years when I was asked to undertake a specific duty that I felt was beneath me. It was a boring task that I didn't want to do. I thought it should have been given to someone else and that I should have been allowed to get on with "real police work". I remember walking into the sergeant's office and asking if I could change the duty that I had been deployed to do. "Why should I give it to someone else in your team?" the sergeant asked. "I'll bring more value doing the other task, and I'll bring more value than [and I named another officer]" I replied. In other words, "I'm too good to serve in the way you've asked me to, and I'm better than that other copper".

That conversation didn't end *quite* as I'd hoped, and my duties for the rest of the week included a lot more of that boring task. But do you see what was going on? I had begun to think of myself more highly than I should have, and that affected my attitude to my service and my response to the person who was deploying me. I felt that I had matured as an officer and grown out of that sort of role, and that I should therefore now be doing other things—more important things.

Isn't that how we often end up thinking as Christians? We can functionally believe that we are beyond the boring and unglamorous aspects of serving. Aren't there younger or newer Christians who can do those things? We can think that what we have going on in our lives trumps what God has called us to in giving our lives for him in service. Aren't there others with more time who are giving less of themselves?

Paul addresses this in Romans 12:3:

> "For by the grace given to me I say to every one among
> you not to think of himself more highly than he
> ought to think, but to think with sober judgement,
> each according to the measure of faith that God has
> assigned."

In other words, be honest in your evaluation of yourself. Remember that you are not the golden child in the kingdom of God and your church—God is not lucky to have you on his team, and you have not earned anything that you have. But, at the same time, remember that you *are* God's child, even when you feel that everything around you is saying the opposite. That's a fact which will never change, regardless of circumstances, gifting, opportunities or feelings.

This is what the gospel does: it helps us see the truth of who we were and who we now are. It reminds us of how Jesus served us: that he humbled himself even to the point of death on a cross (Philippians 2). It reminds us that because of his resurrection, we are not only God's children but co-heirs with Christ, and that we have an amazing inheritance kept for us. It reminds us that as his church, God calls us to lives of service, whether exciting or mundane, which display his glory to the world.

The gospel tells us that we have a contribution to make— we are not to think of ourselves in too lowly a way. And the gospel tells us that no service is beneath us—we are not to think of ourselves in too high a way. The gospel helps us think of ourselves rightly—to be honest and accurate in our self-evaluation.

It is worth pausing here to ask yourself: *have I forgotten this?* Without the sober judgement of thinking of ourselves in terms of the gospel, we risk very quickly becoming half-hearted, growing proud or resentful, or feeling lazy or useless. And if that is how you feel about serving, friend, then you need to come back to the gospel; you need to remember what got you started in the Christian life in the first place. You need to remember who God is, what he has done for you and who you now are in him.

The gospel is not just how we begin the Christian life; it's how we continue it. And it is not only what motivates us to start serving; it's what sustains us to continue serving.

FAITHFUL SERVICE LOOKS LIKE JESUS

"For even the Son of Man came not to be served but to serve, and to give his life as a ransom for many."

(Mark 10:45)

Jesus' ultimate act of service was the lowering of himself to death on a cross to redeem us. But his whole life and ministry here on earth was marked by service. The Gospels are full of stories, incidents and encounters in which Jesus gets down and serves.

When we look at Jesus, we see an overflow of love, humility and joy which sustained his service even in suffering:

- Filled with compassion and love, he raised from the dead the only son of a mourning widow (Luke 7:11-17).

- He did the unthinkable and touched and healed a leper (Matthew 8:1-4).

- He welcomed in a prostitute and allowed her to touch him (Luke 7:36-50).

- In humility, he washed the dirt off the feet of his disciples (John 13:1-17).

- For the joy set before him, he undeservedly died a criminal's death in the place of guilty people (Hebrews 12:2), while asking his Father in heaven to forgive them (Luke 23:34).

I could go on. Read a Gospel sometime and notice and reflect on each way that you see Jesus serving others. And then consider that Jesus told his followers, "A servant is not greater than his master ... If you know these things, blessed are you if you do them" (John 13:16-17). The point is that Jesus is our great example of a true servant of others, and what sustained Jesus—a love for his Father, his people and his world—is what will sustain us too.

Let's use these stories as lenses through which we can zoom in on our hearts to see what is happening inside as we serve. What is motivating us? What is sustaining us?

SERVICE IN LOVE

Jesus loved his Father, and Jesus loved people. It was his compassion that brought him from heaven to earth, and from there to the cross. It is love that matters most:

"If I speak in the tongues of men and of angels, but have not love, I am a noisy gong or a clanging cymbal. And if I have prophetic powers, and understand all mysteries and all knowledge, and if I have all faith, so as to remove mountains, but have not love, I am nothing. If I give away all I have, and if I deliver up my body to be burned, but have not love, I gain nothing."

(1 Corinthians 13:1-3)

In this section of Paul's first letter to the church in Corinth, he is talking about using the gifts God has given us. He is adamant that even if you're the smartest person who understands everything in church, or you have faith that moves Mount Everest, without love you are basically a big, loud noise that no one wants to hear; you achieve nothing.

Service without love will eventually make you feel like you are wading through treacle. It breeds resentment, entitlement and pride, and then it doesn't matter what you do. You could have the most beautiful singing voice and serve in church every week, but without love, from God's perspective you'll be like a donkey screaming— and no one wants to hear that!

In your service for God, the church and the world, let it flow from genuine love (Romans 12:9). How do you do that? By looking at Jesus and asking him to be at work in you by his Spirit. Read a Gospel and look at how Jesus loves you, and how kind and gentle and courageous and compassionate he is. Look at what our spiritual ancestors called his "excellencies". Look at him, and ask him to stir up love as you do so. Then you will find yourself loving him in response.

SERVICE IN HUMILITY

I get to serve God's people as a pastor and to write this for your encouragement (I hope), not because I've figured out how to be a great pastor and writer (I haven't), but all because of his grace. It's not just our salvation that's an unearned gift, but everything we have and use in service to him.

I need to remember that the Lord Jesus served by washing the dirt off his disciples' feet (John 13:1-17). He made himself nothing and took "the very nature of a servant" and was willing to face a horrific criminal's death for me, in obedience to his Father (Philippians 2:5-8, NIV). Humility in service means sacrificially putting the interests of others above our own.

Humble service looks like it sounds—servant-like; we're not afraid to get our hands dirty, not looking for recognition. It's knowing that all our ability to serve is a gift of grace, and we have no reason to feel pride.

SERVICE IN SUFFERING

If our service is to look like Jesus' service, we can guarantee there will be suffering involved. The writer to the Hebrews tells his readers to look to Jesus for help in continuing to strive and live for him. But he reminds them that Jesus "endured the cross", despising shame in his service to God and his people (Hebrews 12:2). Jesus himself promised us that...

> "Whoever wants to be my disciple must deny themselves and take up their cross daily and follow me."
>
> (Luke 9:23)

In the words of my friend, the pastor and author Dai Hankey, as we follow and serve Jesus, "We are to carry a cross, not a cushion".

Faithful service to God will bring suffering—be it the suffering of persecution or the more ordinary costliness of service that takes us out of our comfort zone or demands our time when we're tired or asks us to do something we don't naturally enjoy. But we can take heart: Jesus will strengthen us to endure and to get to the end. The writer to the Hebrews goes on to encourage us to "consider him who endured from sinners such hostility against himself, so that you may not grow weary or faint-hearted" (12:3). Again, as we keep our eyes on Jesus, we will be able to despise the shame of weak commitment and service that looks foolish in the world's eyes.

Following the route our Saviour took will not be pain-free, but it will produce "the peaceful fruit of righteousness" (v 11).

We know service that reflects Jesus will bring suffering, but it doesn't end there...

SERVICE IN JOY

Why did Jesus endure the cross? Why did he despise the shame? Hebrews tells us that it was because of the joy that was set before him (v 2). It was the joy of what his sacrificial servanthood would accomplish: the salvation of sinners—the securing of an eternal inheritance for those he loved that will never fade.

We know joy when we realise what it took for us to have any part in serving our Creator and Redeemer. And we know the joy of what God is doing in us and through us as we serve—displaying his glory to the world (John 15:8, 11, 16). The joy of knowing Jesus, and knowing that somehow he is weaving our work into his purposes, endures whatever the circumstances, whatever the mundanity and whatever the outcome. Even when the pain of the moment is blinding us, we know that eternal joy is awaiting us when we reach the prize that we are pressing on towards (Philippians 3:14; John 16:20-22).

Service that is modelled on Jesus will be manifested in unspeakable joy.

UNFAITHFUL SERVICE

So that's what faithful service looks like. But there is such a thing as unfaithful service. What does that look like? We're given an example in the parable of the talents in Luke 19:11-27.

It goes like this: a nobleman has to leave his country to receive a kingdom. Before he sets off, he gathers ten of his servants and gives them each a portion of his treasure (a mina—about three months' wages) to do business on his behalf while he is away. So the man leaves, is crowned as king and then returns to his country. On his return, he starts making enquiries about his business affairs and the work of his servants. Calling them in, he's made aware of two servants who have been successful with the portion of treasure that he had left them to manage. One has increased the mina ten times and the other five times. The king is delighted and rewards them with what appears to be a disproportionate bonus—one will have authority over ten cities and the other over five. But then he speaks to a third servant, and his report could not be more different. This servant stands before the king with the mina in his hand, reporting that he kept it wrapped in a handkerchief and buried in the ground. Before the king can ask why, the servant just comes out with it: "I was afraid of you, because you are a severe man. You take what you did not deposit, and reap what you did not sow" (v 21).

Why did the servant believe this about the nobleman, when he was clearly a generous master who rewarded his servants richly for their work? The clue might be found in verse 14:

> "But his citizens hated him and sent a delegation after
> him, saying, 'We do not want this man to reign over us.'"

It sounds as if the unfaithful servant had forgotten his role and duty to the king as servant, and instead had been influenced by the citizens' feelings and believed their lies. Or maybe the servant's excuses were exactly that—excuses—because if he had really been afraid, surely he would have at least put the money in the bank and made some interest. His defensive words condemned him as a wicked servant, and as a result he was left with nothing. He didn't do business because he didn't love the king. He didn't value what he had been given, and he didn't value the one who had asked him to serve.

Unfaithful service is what happens when we don't love our King, Jesus. We believe lies about him, we forget who he has made us to be, and we lose sight of the value of what he has given us. Our unfaithfulness in service could be passivity, as with this servant—or doing the bare minimum, serving in the way that maintains the most possible comfort and requires the least possible sacrifice. Alternatively, it could be doing a lot... but with a grumbling heart, a self-righteous spirit or an entitled attitude. It is an approach to serving that means we're making it all about us rather than about God or other people:

"Do people realise how long I have been here for?"

"Where is everyone? I've left my family at home to do this."

"No one notices what I do for this place."

"If I wasn't here this church would fall apart."

These are all things I have thought or even said at times over the years. They have not pleased my Saviour, and they have robbed me of the joy of serving God and his church. But then I have to remember that I am saved by grace, not through my work or my attitude to my work. There is always forgiveness and a fresh start, and God's Spirit is at work to reorient our motivations back to faithfulness and love.

Jesus has ascended to be with the Father, and one day he will return. While we await that return, we do business on his behalf with the portion of treasure that he has given us. We put to use the time, gifts and opportunities he has given us, to serve the church and the world, which so desperately needs him, and we do it gladly because we're doing it for him. We do it each day, sustained by the gospel, following the example of Jesus, knowing that we're getting nearer to the day when we will meet him. By grace he will welcome us in, and for each act of humble, willing, loving service, he will say, "Well done, good and faithful servant". That thought is enough to sustain us in our serving!

ACTION STEPS

- What would your service to God, the church and the world look like if it was motivated, sustained, and grounded in gospel truth and love for Jesus?

- Spend time thinking and praying through where your heart is when it comes to serving in terms of love, humility, suffering and joy.

- Are there areas in your service to God where you know you struggle with being self-centred, self-protective or self-exalting? Spend time repenting in prayer, knowing that your Saviour Jesus will forgive, encourage and comfort you.

4. SERVE AS THE PERSON GOD HAS MADE YOU TO BE

"This is not very good, is it, Steven? What are you going to do with your life now?"

That's what my headteacher said to me as I sat in his office on a hot August morning in 1997. It was A-level results day, and the sweat dripped down my back as I gazed down at the grades I had "achieved".

Sociology: N

General Studies: N

Geography: U

Economics: U

If you're wondering what those grades mean… "U" stands for unclassified and "N" for non-classified. I have no clue about what I did to climb from a U (which is the lowest grade) to an N (which is the next grade up) in two of the subjects. Maybe I spelled my name right at the top of the paper. I'm not sure. I like to think of those grades as two "unlucky's" and two "nearly there's".

I share this because, since that moment, I have wrestled daily with the temptation of defining who I am, how I live and how I serve according to those four letters. My level of academic prowess (which has not improved much since that day) has sometimes defined my thinking and at times has stopped me serving God and others well. But these insecurities also tempt me to glorify myself when I do serve in the same way as people who have more degrees than Fahrenheit. The crux of the issue is this: my instinct is to think that in order to serve God and his people well, I need to bring something to the table. I need what others have. At times I still think God didn't get it right with me. If he'd made things go a little differently—if those two "Ns" had been two "Es"—that would have given me a shot at university, and (I tell myself) I could have been more of an asset to the church and God's kingdom. If only I were, well, someone different, I'd be so much more useful as a servant of God.

Is this how you feel when it comes to your life? Is this how it feels when you think about serving God and your church? Most of us look at other people and know they're better than us—academically, or in terms of confidence, or speaking ability, or simple strength, or musical gifts, or energy, or ability to make friends, or whatever. And then we can easily conclude that God could use me if I was like another person, but because I'm not, I'm not much use.

The world will tell us that what we need to do is just to realise how brilliant we really are (or maybe you're already there—you do think you bring a lot to God's table). But the Bible says that the answer to feeling too weak or unable to serve is not to try to feel strong...

YOU ARE NOT DEFINED BY WHAT YOU BRING TO THE TABLE

"For you formed my inward parts;
you knitted me together in my mother's womb.
I praise you, for I am fearfully and wonderfully made.
Wonderful are your works;
my soul knows it very well.
My frame was not hidden from you,
when I was being made in secret,
intricately woven in the depths of the earth.
Your eyes saw my unformed substance;
in your book were written, every one of them,
the days that were formed for me,
when as yet there was none of them."

(Psalm 139:13-16)

In this psalm, King David is marvelling over the mind-blowing process of how he was formed in his mother's womb (v 13) and praising God that before he was even created, his life had been planned for him and written in God's book (v 16).

Friend, that is true for you no less than it was for David. You are fearfully and wonderfully made, and God, in his sovereignty, planned your days before the foundation of the world. Before all things were created, he had set his affections on you and predestined you to be holy and blameless before him (Ephesians 1:3-6). Before you were even a twinkle in your mother's and father's eyes, your heavenly Father had laid a place at his family table for you. You are not defined by what you do or do not bring to the table; you are defined by the fact that the one who created you and has your days within his hands has invited you to the table because of his Son, Jesus.

God wants you and me to serve as the people he has made us to be. The only living sacrifice I can give is *my* life, not someone else's. *My* life, with all its imperfections, weaknesses, experiences, moments and gifts. What you bring to the table of the kingdom is you! You are a member of the body of Christ (Romans 12:4-5), who has been given gifts of the Spirit for the benefit of the whole church (1 Corinthians 12:4-7).

Who God has made you to be is deliberate! And it's the primary means by which you can serve. The life he has given you is the foundation for how you will best serve him, his church and the world. He does not make mistakes. You can truly serve him with all your personal experiences and even your weaknesses.

YOU CAN SERVE FROM YOUR EXPERIENCES

Roy is one of our church's former elders. He is 78, and recently he shared with my co-pastor Paul that he couldn't wait to be 80. Why?

"Because Moses did his best work for God when he was 80."

This got me thinking about how God used the experiences of Moses's long life to enable him to serve.

Moses's birth could not have been much more traumatic. He was born right in the middle of a genocide, committed by the means of infanticide, commanded by a wicked and insecure pharaoh. Moses' mother, Jochebed, kept her baby boy a secret for three months and then placed him in a basket, made it as watertight as she could and placed him in the reeds at the bank of the River Nile, sending her daughter, Miriam, to see what would happen to him.

What came next was the worst thing they could have imagined. Who discovered the baby? Pharaoh's daughter—the daughter of the man who had given the command that every little Hebrew baby boy should die. She recognised him as a Hebrew child (Exodus 2:6)... but rather than obey her father's orders, she felt compassion for him and responded well to the baby's sister bravely offering to find a nanny to nurse and care for the baby— his own mother, who nursed him probably for two or three years. During that period, he would have spent time among his people, hearing about God, until he was old enough to be returned to Pharaoh's daughter, who adopted him.

This was the start of Moses' life experience, which God would use for his purposes.

"And Moses was instructed in all the wisdom of the Egyptians, and he was mighty in his words and deeds" (Acts 7:22). Moses' upbringing gave him an education in the world of the Egyptians, whom he would have to face in years to come. As he grew older, his compassion for the Hebrew people grew to the point where he took matters into his own hands and killed a man who was beating a fellow Hebrew (Exodus 2:11-12). Needing to flee from Egypt, he lost not only his privileges and relationships but also the respect of the people whom he would one day lead (v 13-15). As far as he was concerned, his life was falling apart. He found himself in the wilderness—a place where there was no food or water, the heat was unbearable, and every day was a struggle. But it was through this experience that we see God further shaping Moses for his service. Moses stepped in to serve and protect the daughters of a Midianite priest. He married one of them, became a shepherd and found himself leading, feeding and protecting sheep, learning the geography of the land through which he would one day need to lead God's people.

The 19th-century American evangelist D.L. Moody once said something along the lines that Moses was 40 years in Egypt learning to be something. He was then 40 years in the wilderness learning to be nothing, so that he could spend 40 years proving God to be everything.

Moses served from the experiences of the life that God had given him. And God also has plans for you. Granted, that may not be leading God's people out of slavery, but no one has lived the life that you have. God has given you, his child, experiences that prepare you for the acts of service he is calling you to. There are no wasted moments; both the good and the bad can be used to serve God and the church. You may have worked in a job that has given you skills that can serve the church. You may have experienced different cultures while travelling, which can help you to reach asylum seekers in your neighbourhood. You may have been married for 30 years, or you may have gone through a divorce, and your experience and wisdom from that time could serve younger couples within your church. You may have children with complex needs and be able to walk alongside other parents in similar situations. You may be disabled and housebound, but you can pray for others and encourage them through texts and phone calls.

Since God has prepared good works for us to walk in (Ephesians 2:10) and also prepared our days before we were even born, surely everything in those days is part of God equipping us for his service. What I love about this is that God can and does redeem the worst of experiences for his glory and our good. As I look back on my own life, I can put my finger on the events that God used to shape and prepare me for serving him and his people. Some of them are fond memories and obvious influences, like having Christian parents, being married to Siân, being a father of four kids, my time in the police force, or working for a Christian relief and development agency. Yet there are other times in my life that God has used but I want to forget. Experiences and circumstances that weigh heavy and are ongoing struggles are things I would not choose, but they are also ways that God is guiding and equipping me in service for him.

"How has, and how is, God shaping and preparing me for service to him and the church?" This has been a helpful question for me to try to answer when reflecting on my life. Why don't you ask yourself the same thing? Spend time thinking, praying and reflecting on your life. God has made you to be you and given you the life you've had, so that you can serve as you.

SERVING FROM YOUR WEAKNESS

How are you this morning?

I'm fine, thank you.

Can I help you with that?

I can manage, thanks.

Do you need anything?

No, I'm good.

In the past hour, I've asked these questions and received these responses from three different people in the coffee shop where I am writing this chapter. The first answer was from someone from church who I know is not fine. The second was from a young mum that I see regularly here. She comes in each morning with three small kids—two in a double stroller and a toddler bouncing around. This morning she was struggling because she'd got the stroller stuck while trying to manoeuvre past some tables. I offered to help, and her answer? "I can manage, thanks." The last question was at the end of a phone call with someone who I know needs help in a certain area, but when I asked, they said they were "good".

Why is this? What is it about us that can't cope with the fact that at times (and for some of us, all the time) we need help? I know that in British culture there's still an unwritten rule that when faced with crisis, difficulty or anything that may spark an emotional response and require help from others, we pull ourselves together, pour ourselves a cup of tea and try to press on, even if we know we can't. But this is not just a British problem; this is a human problem. When I talk about weakness here, I don't mean sin but rather our frailties—the ways in which we need God and other people. When it comes to our weaknesses, we have a tendency not to accept them, but instead we apologise for them and even repent of them. So we end up either trying to serve out of our own (limited) strength or thinking that our areas of weakness make us unfit to serve at all.

But the Bible speaks of weakness in a very different way. Let's return to Moses...

They will not believe me...

I can't do it...

Please send someone else...

When God called Moses to return to Egypt and lead his people out of slavery, he was immediately filled with doubt, fear and dread. His first reaction was "Who am I that I should go to Pharaoh and bring the children of Israel out of Egypt?" (Exodus 3:11). Have you ever felt similar emotions when faced with serving in a way that you just don't feel qualified for? Look at Moses' three responses to God.

THEY WILL NOT BELIEVE ME...

At first glance, this is a reasonable assumption (4:1). Before Moses fled from Egypt, the last thing he had heard from one of the Hebrew people was "Who made you a prince and a judge over us?" (2:14). As far as Moses is concerned, unless the people truly believe that God has met with him, they are not going to listen. Moses fears his past reputation will disqualify him, even though God has already told him, "They will listen to your voice" (3:18).

Look at my past, says Moses. *Do you see what a weakness that is? I can't do this!*

God's response to Moses is gracious. He gives him three signs that will prove to the Hebrews that Moses has been with God and act as warnings to Egypt, as well as showing Moses that his weaknesses are not barriers to serving God.

Ok, Moses, you want a sign? says God. *Let me show you what I can do with a stick.* God instructs Moses to throw his staff on the ground, and it turns into a serpent (4:2-5). God then tells him to put out his hand and catch it by the tail, and as he does, the snake turns back into a staff. It is as if God is saying, *If I can do that with a lifeless stick, imagine what I can do with the hand that holds it.*

I CAN'T DO IT...

After the snake, Moses is given two more miraculous signs, but he's ready with his next excuse. *I'm not eloquent—I've never been eloquent, and I'm slow of speech* (v 10). Moses seems to have had a genuine issue—whether that was a speech impediment or a fear of public speaking we don't know. But whatever it was, Moses saw it as something that would stop him from doing what God was asking him to do. But God's response is amazing:

> "Then the LORD said to him, 'Who has made man's mouth? Who makes him mute, or deaf, or seeing, or blind? Is it not I, the LORD? Now therefore go, and I will be with your mouth and teach you what you shall speak.'" (v 11-12)

It's as if God is saying, *I know how I have made you, Moses; and it's in and through that weakness that I will work—so go and serve me.*

PLEASE SEND SOMEONE ELSE...

Reading Moses' responses here is like watching my kids try to refuse point-blank to do something even when all the excuses and reasons for them not doing it have been removed. It is at this point that Moses' real reason comes out, which is basically *I just don't want to do it... Please send someone else* (v 13). But again we see the patience and grace of God, who, rather than strike Moses down or write him off, gives him someone to help him: his brother, Aaron. Aaron will hear from Moses, who will hear from God, and Aaron will then speak.

Have you ever been faced with a task and thought, "Why me?" as you imagine all the people you think could do a better job? Have you felt disqualified because of past mistakes or noticeable flaws? Moses assumed that the shame of his past and his struggle to speak meant he couldn't serve in the way God had called him to. God had to show him that his weaknesses need not be barriers to his service.

DON'T REPENT OF WEAKNESS—EMBRACE IT!

Not serving God because of our weakness and perceived inabilities is a complete misunderstanding of how God works and how he is glorified through us. In the Gospel of John, regarding a man who had been born blind,

Jesus' disciples asked, "Rabbi, who sinned, this man or his parents, that he was born blind?" (John 9:2). Jesus replied that it was neither—the man was born blind so that the works of God might be displayed in him.

The apostle Paul was accused, by the church in Corinth, of having no presence and not being able to speak well, yet God worked through him to such an extent that he was the greatest evangelist and church planter who has ever lived. He explained that, as Christians, we hold the treasure of the gospel within us (2 Corinthians 4:5-7), but we are like jars of clay—we are weak, we crack, we can be damaged. Yet amazingly, God uses these fragile jars, and in doing so, he shows that the power belongs to him and not to us.

It blows my mind to know that the power of God is mysteriously seen in the inadequacies and weaknesses of the people whom he uses for his service and his glory. That's why Paul could say, "If I must boast, I will boast of the things that show my weakness" (11:30). So don't be disappointed with your weakness or apologise for your weakness or try to cover up your weakness; rather embrace your weakness. Failing to understand and accept the fact that you can't serve God in your own strength will hinder your service for him and his people. Be thankful, like Paul, and serve from a position of embracing your weakness:

> "I will boast all the more gladly of my weaknesses, so
> that the power of Christ may rest upon me. For the

sake of Christ, then, I am content with weaknesses,
insults, hardships, persecutions, and calamities. For
when I am weak, then I am strong." (12:9-10)

My mum, Pauline, is disabled. On the day after my
parents' wedding, they were in a car accident that
resulted in her fracturing her neck. This has developed
into a degenerative disorder that, over time, has put
her in a wheelchair and left her unable to leave her
house without help. She is unable to serve in church
in the conventional ways, often spending hours on her
own. But despite what has happened to her, she serves
God, his people and the world. She spends time calling
people to encourage them; she creates craft resources
for a local charity which is reaching Muslim women with
the gospel; people come to visit and encourage her, but
instead they leave built up in the Lord because of her.
And she prays—for hours she prays.

I recall a time when she was particularly sad about her
health situation. The reality of her life and the frustration
of her weaknesses were particularly prominent in her
thoughts at that time. In the midst of her tears, I was able
to share with her the names of numerous people she had
served, loved, prayed for and led to Christ—including
her own five children. What will always stay with me is
her response: "Lots of those things I would never have
done if I didn't have my disability, son". In that moment,
through the cloud of sadness, my mum understood (and
taught me) what it means to serve as the person God has

made us to be—in accordance with the days that he has planned for us, the experiences he has given us and the weakness he sovereignly uses for his glory, for his church and for our good.

What goes for Moses, Paul and my mum goes for me and you too. You are who God has made you to be, and while you are limited, he is not. Don't let your sense of your own shortcomings or inabilities stop you from stepping out and serving him in the ways he's calling you to. For when you are weak, you are also strong—because he is.

ACTION STEPS

- Spend time reflecting on your life experiences, asking God to reveal to you the evidence of his grace in significant moments. How has God used those moments to shape you? If you are struggling, ask a friend or church leader to talk it through with you.

- Ask God to help you see how you can use these experiences to serve him.

- What area of weakness are you resenting and not embracing? What area of service are you seeking to do in your own strength because of this? What area of service are you not stepping into because of this weakness?

5. SERVE WITH WHAT GOD
HAS GIVEN YOU

The great debate before the 2022 football World Cup was: who is the greatest football player in the world? Argentina's Lionel Messi or Portugal's talisman, Cristiano Ronaldo? Both had won numerous team and personal trophies; both had scored hundreds of goals; but neither had lifted the World Cup, experiencing disappointment time and time again in that competition.

This time it ended very differently for these two men. Portugal were eliminated in the quarter finals, with Ronaldo not even making the starting line-up because of his attitude at being substituted in the previous round, whereas Messi victoriously lifted the trophy while being exalted in the world of football punditry as the GOAT— the Greatest Of All Time.

But we're talking about a team game, not an individual sport like boxing or tennis. Football is a game where everyone in the team is necessary: the defence need the attack and vice versa, and the players who provide the assists are just as important as the players that score the goals. The Argentinian team was made up of different levels of giftedness—different strengths. It contained players that most people had never heard of as well as the greatest player of all time. Those teammates worked for each other, supported one another, covered for one another when mistakes were made and honoured each other when they were victorious. Despite his individual genius, Messi was never going to win without his team. He and his team knew that, regardless of the media frenzy, and that's what made the difference and brought the victory.

Serving the church is not an individual endeavour; it's a team game. We are all part of the team—none of us are spectators watching from the stands. And we all have different God-given strengths, and we are to use them to serve one another and to invite others to join the team while bringing glory to our victorious King, Jesus.

GIFTS FROM GOD

"Having gifts that differ according to the grace given to us, let us use them." (Romans 12:6)

"To each is given the manifestation of the Spirit for the common good." (1 Corinthians 12:7)

As we saw in chapters 1 and 2 of this book, Paul encourages us to offer our whole lives sacrificially in view of what Jesus has done for us; and as we explored in chapter 3, we please God as we respond rightly and rationally to his grace and mercy (Romans 12:1). The gospel enables us to think of ourselves accurately (with sober judgement, v 3), recognising that we have not earned anything that God has given us—which deals with our issue of pride—but also that God has gifted us for his purpose—which deals with false modesty and feelings of having nothing to offer. Having covered this ground, Paul gives the context in which all this is primarily to be lived out and realised: the local church. In verse 4 he describes the church using the metaphor of the body:

> "For as in one body we have many members, and the members do not all have the same function, so we, though many, are one body in Christ, and individually members one of another." (v 4-5)

As we explored in the previous chapter, our different experiences shape and inform who we are and what we can bring to serve God and his church—and it's also true of our different gifts. My ear has the specialised God-given ability to open my body to the wonder of sound, my eye is the gateway that enables me to see the beauty of God's creation, and my feet take me on the journey of experiencing life. None of these body parts can do what the others can; each of them needs the others. Similarly, part of giving yourself as a living sacrifice is to play your distinctive part in serving your church with the gifts that God has given you. These gifts are the manifestation of the Spirit—using them testifies to the power of God's grace in our lives. Paul says in both Romans 12 and 1 Corinthians 12 that we are given these gifts for the common good of the church: for building up other church members.

GIFTS OF GOD

So, what are these gifts? In Romans 12:6-8 Paul lists a number of them, making clear that all of us get at least one of them but that none of us get all of them.

"Having gifts that differ according to the grace given to us, let us use them." (v 6)

We are not a team of Messis or a band of John Lennons; we are a group of people who are each unique. The different gifts are not randomly assigned but are given according to God's grace. So, just as a World Cup-winning team has players in different positions who are gifted in different aspects of the game, and a successful band has musicians who are gifted in playing different instruments, we perform best when we use the specific gifts that God has given us.

In Romans 12, Paul lists the following gifts: prophecy, service, teaching, exhorting, giving, leading and acts of mercy. In 1 Corinthians 12:7-10 he mentions, in addition, the gifts of wisdom, knowledge, faith[1], gifts of healing, working of miracles, prophecy, the ability to

---

1 Not the faith we're to have in Christ for salvation but a specific faith for a particular task or circumstance.

distinguish between spirits, various kinds of tongues and the interpretation of tongues. In verse 28 we also read about the gifts of helping and administration. Paul explains that God gives some gifts so that people can take up specific roles in the building up of the church. The roles listed in verse 29 are apostles, prophets and teachers, and in Ephesians 4:11-12 he also lists evangelists and pastors/shepherds, who are to equip the church for ministry.

All the gifts mentioned in the New Testament can be loosely placed into three categories: the first two categories are the gifts of speaking (often seen publicly) and gifts of serving (the gifts often done in private) (1 Peter 4:11). Every gift, including speaking, is a form of serving God and the church. The gifts of speaking are often self-explanatory, like preaching, Bible teaching, leading a Bible study, counselling, evangelism, music and so on. The gifts of serving are the things that are often not seen but are vital to the life of the church, such as (in a typical 21st-century church) the church accounts, administration, hospital visits, cleaning, moving chairs, giving gifts, making meals, opening your home, funding projects, praying, audio visual skills... The list is endless.

The third category, mentioned in Ephesians 4, highlights what we could label "gifts of influence" in the church:

"And he gave the apostles, the prophets, the evangelists, the shepherds and teachers, to equip the saints for the

*work of ministry, for building up the body of Christ,
until we all attain to the unity of the faith and of the
knowledge of the Son of God, to mature manhood, to
the measure of the stature of the fullness of Christ."*

(v 11–13)

These serving-through-leading roles are given by God to create the environment for others to flourish in (and certainly not as an opportunity to lord it over the rest of the church). We often wrongly assume that these kinds of roles put a person in a higher echelon and means they don't have any of the behind-the-scenes gifts or shouldn't engage in less "glamorous" areas of service. But this couldn't be more wrong—it was the Lord Jesus who washed feet, touched lepers, broke bread, cooked breakfast and said that to be great in his kingdom, you must be a servant like him (Matthew 20:26-28). Any gift of leadership or influence is about serving others.

We shouldn't assume that pastors and full-time Christian workers are the only people of influence in the church when it comes to equipping the saints for ministry. My church runs a training track called Equip (original, I know), and the sessions that cover areas like evangelism, biblical counselling and theology are usually delivered by church members who are not part of the leadership team but have gifts in these areas. As they teach others, they grow in their gifting and people benefit from their example.

YOUR GIFT IS A GOOD GIFT

Let's recap a few things that we have seen so far.

- What you bring to the table is not what defines you. You have a place at the table of God because of his Son, Jesus.

- You have been wonderfully, uniquely made by God to be you, with all your experiences and weaknesses.

- You are not the silver bullet for your church's problems; equally, you are needed by your church.

- The best gift that you bring to your church is you.

- Any gift you have is given by God for the building up of others (the church) and for his glory.

It is crucial to remember this last, foundational point because, sadly, in my own experience, as soon as I start thinking about gifting, a sizeable foothold appears for the devil to stand on. I either start getting puffed up with pride and praise for myself or I start to think I am useless and have little to offer. Thinking of myself with sober judgement goes out of the window.

It is also important for some of us to remember that everyone is gifted; the Holy Spirit hasn't left anyone out: "*To each is given* the manifestation of the Spirit for the common good" (1 Corinthians 12:7, emphasis added; see also 1 Peter 4:10).

All believers—yes, even you—have received at least one gift from God, and we are to use that gift to serve others. That means that no one, including you, has nothing to offer. It also means that no one is in a position where they don't need others. We all rely on other people's gifts to build a healthy, thriving church.

One of the big difficulties we encounter when thinking through how God has gifted us is that we view certain gifts as being more worthy than others, and therefore we see the people who hold certain gifts as more worthy than other people. We see gifts on a spectrum from "most worthy"—perhaps preaching, speaking in tongues or leading worship (often, the gifts that are more "on show" are those that are elevated)—to the "less worthy" ones like administration or generosity (unseen gifts). But while a church will die over a generation because of bad theology and preaching, it can die virtually overnight because of bad administration. This misguided view sometimes arises because our understanding of what matters in church has been shrunk down to what happens up front in a service. But the lists of gifts that God gives his people are not exhaustive, and they are not limited to a couple of hours on a Sunday, far less to what happens on the stage at the front in those hours; they're exercised every day of the week in countless situations for the building up of his people.

God gives certain gifts to the church that edify the church in ways that other gifts are not able to do; and Paul tells the church in Corinth that they should earnestly desire those gifts—the ones which most build up the church, especially prophecy (1 Corinthians 14:1).[2] But, to underline the point, he does not say that the people who have those gifts are more worthy than anyone else in the church.

HOW DO I DISCOVER MY GIFTS?

"I'm not gifted."

"I have nothing to offer."

"I couldn't do that."

When we're trying to discern how God has gifted us and how he wants us to use that gifting, discouraging thoughts like these can flood in and stop us from even taking the first step. Sometimes we are tempted to compare ourselves with others, and we feel discouraged. But sometimes we simply just don't know how to discern our gifts. As churches, we need to get better at helping people discover how they may be gifted, and at encouraging each other to dare to use those gifts.

---

2 Bible-teaching churches land on different definitions of what this gift is today, so I have chosen not to be too definite for the sake of unity; but for what it's worth, we at Cornerstone Church Liverpool hold that what Paul says in 1 Corinthians 14 (to desire spiritual gifts, especially prophecy) is a command rather than a statement. And we define prophecy to be the speaking forth in merely human words of something God has spontaneously brought to mind for the building up of the church. All of this is to be tested and interpreted according to and under the authority of Scripture.

In Tim Keller's comments on Romans 12 in *Romans 8 – 16 For You*, he suggests that there are at least two ways to help you discern your gifting.[3]

The first is *self-examination*—to think of yourself with sober judgment enables you to ask yourself honest questions: What do I enjoy doing? Am I good at what I enjoy? What are the things that I notice? What are the things that capture my attention, both the problems and the opportunities? Who am I drawn to speak to? Is it newcomers? Older people? What am I good at?

As a start, write these questions out and then ask God to help you answer them over the course of a week. This will begin to give you an idea of the things that spark your interest and affections, and that could unearth gifts you can use to serve.

The second thing that Keller suggests is *experience*—you need to experience different ministries in the church before you can recognise what your gifts might be. You don't know if you are gifted at teaching children till you open the Bible with them a few times; you don't know if you have an aptitude for administration in the life of the church till you offer to punch numbers into a spreadsheet; you don't know if you love meeting new people and should become part of the welcome team till you chat to a visitor; you don't know if you have the gift of hospitality till you open up your life and home

---

3 *Romans 8-16 For You* (The Good Book Company, 2015), p 113-114.

to others. In considering Paul's statement about "using" your gift, Keller suggests you need to start serving in different ministries to find out if you have the gifts to serve in those areas. (And it's fine if the answer is no!)

As well as writing the answers to the questions that you ask yourself, spend time studying the biblical lists of gifts to help yourself process which areas you have or don't have experience in, and to guide biblically some of the answers to your self-examination questions.

I want to add a third way to discern your gifts, which I think is vital: *seeking the wisdom of others.*

My wife, Siân, is in the middle of undertaking a course in biblical counselling. One of the assignments required her to ask people from our church family about her gifts. As many people would, she found it uncomfortable to ask others to share how they felt God had gifted her, but the responses she received were surprising, encouraging and affirming. Surprising because people identified things in Siân of which she had been unaware. Encouraging because people picked up on things that Siân was good at that I had already been encouraging her to step further into. And affirming because the very reason she was doing the course was because she believed God wanted to develop her gift of walking alongside people. The exercise both helped her and in turn blessed others as she stepped into these areas of gifting and service.

In the Acts 29 church-planting network, which I'm part of, we walk alongside churches who are planning new church plants. One way we do that is to assess the church planters—not as if for a school examination but by helping the planter, his wife (if he has one) and the sending church to affirm his gifting and calling. Every time I have the privilege of being part of an assessment, I am always encouraged to see the sense of discovery and the clarity that those being assessed experience from asking others for their perspectives.

Let me encourage you to ask your church—the leaders, your small-group leaders and fellow church members—to help you discover your gifts. Ask them:

- *How do you see me serving God and the church?*

- *In what ways do you discern that has God gifted me?*

- *Are there areas of service that you think I should explore more?*

If your church has structured ways of doing this, I'd encourage you to step into those. If you feel you have clarity on how God has gifted you or have a desire to grow in certain gifts, I'd suggest you speak with your church leaders. Our gifts and calling are affirmed by God through his people, so it's a good idea to figure it out with the church, not on our own. Don't be a "self-proclaimed" anything—seek to be a humble servant, who is willing to submit and be guided and supported as you seek to serve God and your church.

GIVE IT A GO

Discerning our gifts is the groundwork, but at the same time, it is healthy to be ready to volunteer where there is a need—even if you don't think that you have the necessary gifts.

Wisdom is necessary here; if the worship team requires a guitarist and you don't play, your "giving it a go" is going to result in a very quick and very public unearthing of your lack of skill. But generally with this mindset of "give it a go", there are so many areas where you can step in to volunteer and needs that you could meet.

As a church leader, I find it really encouraging (and I can't imagine how much it delights our heavenly Father) when someone says, "I'm not sure if I'd be any good at that, but I can see there's a need, and I'll give it a go".

Gifting can be discovered when we step in to meet a need, but it's also in meeting needs that the heart of service is fostered. This cultivates an attitude to serving which is primarily about giving, not gifting—about knowing that the Lord has called us to give ourselves for his glory and for the sake of others in the body. This kind of sacrificial service is what we see in Jesus. It overrides the self-centred attitude of only doing what we think we're good at or what satisfies us personally. Dying on the cross was not Jesus' speciality skill as such, nor was washing feet at the top of his list of aptitudes, but he served in those ways out of his love for us and for the glory of his Father.

So, next time you spot a need or hear the call for volunteers, step in and give it a go.

WHAT AM I DOING NOW?

So often, discussions about finding your gifting end up being about what you can do in the future rather than what you are doing now. We easily miss what we are already doing that is of service to God and his people.

I remember having a conversation with a member of our church who was struggling to figure out how best she could serve. To me, her gifts were obvious: she was amazing at making new people feel at home in our church. She is a brilliant conversationalist and amazingly aware of the needs of people during our services. I could see this, but she couldn't. Without telling her what I thought, I encouraged her to pray, asking God to open her eyes to how she was serving. When she did pray, God showed her not only how she served on a Sunday but also throughout the whole week, which filled her with great joy and enhanced her service even more.

So, even as you consider how you might be gifted and what you might step into that's new for you, be also asking God to open your eyes to see how you are already serving him and his people.

WHAT HAS HE GIVEN ME?

When I was kid, we used to listen to a set of cassette tapes (which dates me!) called *Kid's Praise*. Each tape featured the main character, Psalty, the singing song book, who would travel around sharing the good news of Jesus with children and young people, teaching them all kinds of praise songs. Our favourite was the one where Psalty took the church youth group camping. During the trip, they meet a Scottish firefly called Farley who can't fly because he only has one wing. The kids introduce Farley to Psalty as "disabled", but Farley quickly jumps in and says, "With the Lord I am more than able. I may not be able to fly, but I can glow, and when I glow, I give the glory all to God." Farley then jumps up onto Psalty's shoulder and lights the way as they hike in the dark.

Farley was aware of what God had given him; despite his inability to fly, he knew that he could glow. His focus was on what he could do, not on what he couldn't; and he seemed a far more joyful firefly because of it.

What are the things God has given you? Maybe you can write. Maybe you can cook or bake. Maybe you have time, or money, or a home. Maybe you have years of experience in accounts, management or teaching children. Maybe you are great at cleaning or DIY. Maybe you are naturally hospitable.[4] You may not be able to sing, or preach, or clean, or have enough money to support others, but there will be a way in which you can glow.

---

4 Hospitality is primarily about having an open life before it is about an open home. Jesus was the most hospitable person to walk the planet, and he never had a home.

We have a number of builders in our church who can plaster walls, rewire houses and plumb in bathrooms. You won't find those particular skills mentioned in the biblical lists of gifts, but the guys in our church are using these gifts to build up people in the church family—through work in our building, doing jobs for church members and employing Christians and non-Christians, using their businesses to disciple some guys and witness to others as they work.

So, what has God given you? Whatever it is, use it for service to him and, like Farley, as you glow, you can give the glory all to God.

CELEBRATING THE GIFTS OF OTHERS

One often missed way that we can serve each other well is to "outdo one another in showing honour" (Romans 12:10). This is the only place in the Bible where we are told to seek to be better than others. Instead of competing against others, we're competing to show them the most honour. This comes straight after Paul has told us to use our gifts and reminded us that our love should be genuine and that we should love our church as our family.

It's no accident that he then says, *Show honour to each other*. We can do this by helping others to discover their gifts and figure out how best they can serve. We can do it by thanking others for the way they use their gifts for the church, by telling others how their serving is making a difference, by praising others for how they are meeting a need, and by telling others how we see Jesus in and through them. We can do it by encouraging both those who are quietly serving usually in unseen ways and those who serve up front and are clearly gifted—those you feel probably don't need your encouragement may well be most in need of it.

When your priority is to love God and others, and when you see that you can never go overboard in showing honour, you will delight in helping others flourish in their gifting and service. In the process you may even find you have the gift of encouragement!

DO IT ALL WITH LOVE

As we saw in chapter 3 of this book, when we looked at 1 Corinthians 13, I could be the most gifted, most sacrificial person—I could even die in service of others— but if I don't have love, I gain nothing, and I give nothing. This is why Paul, straight after calling the Christians in Corinth to desire the gifts that can build up the church the most, tells them that he "will show [them] a still more excellent way" (12:31). And the most excellent way is not so much about what we do but how we do it—in love. The use of our gifts should be kind, not boastful, not arrogant, not resentful, but bearing all things and believing all things, hoping all things and enduring all things—and never ending (13:4-8).

It is love that will drive and sustain your service. It is love that will see you use your gifts genuinely for the good of your church rather than for your own ends or to win yourself praise. In love God gave you your gifts; in love you are to use them for his people.

Each morning Siân and I do a short devotion with our kids. (Before you picture a perfect Christian family scene with children fully engaged in repeating verses of the New Testament in Greek, I can assure you that these times often include some kids falling asleep in their breakfast cereal while others run around the kitchen trying to find their homework books.) One thing I always try and do at the end, before sending them off to school, is to pray this:

"Lord, please help us to love you and love people well today."

I know that only a God-given love for him and for other people will cause me and my family to serve others throughout the day. Love will be the trigger to help us see the need and give us the desire to serve. Service is not about us. And genuine service only comes from genuine love, so when you are trying to discover your gifts or stepping up to meet a need, you could do worse than to start with this prayer:

"Lord, please help me love you and love people well in this."

ACTION STEPS

- "You are not the silver bullet for your church's problems; equally, you are needed by your church." Are you more likely to stray into thinking you are a "silver bullet", or that you are not really needed by your church? What difference to your serving would either of those mistakes make?

- Are there gifts that, personally or as a church, you tend to view or treat as being more worthy than others? How can you proactively, in your thinking, praying, and actions, counteract this?

- Spend time working through the three ways to discern your gifting that this chapter lays out:
  1. Self-examination
  2. Experience
  3. Seeking wisdom (use the questions on p 82)

- Think of two or three fellow church members who you can show honour to by telling them what difference their serving makes to your church—and then do so!

6. SERVE WHERE GOD HAS PLACED YOU

Two of the biggest barriers to effective service are our tendency to wait for what's next and to look back at what's gone, instead of getting on with life in the present.

In November 2009, I went to Ramilies Road Chapel (which became Cornerstone Church) with a small group of people to work in partnership with the existing congregation to replant the church. The chapel had been a once thriving Brethren Assembly, but by then had only 15 people attending on a Sunday, an ageing congregation and a growing anxiety that the church that had been part of their lives for over 50 years was perhaps about to close. They knew their situation, and they wanted to see their church used by God to reach the thousands of people in the area who did not know Jesus, but they were stuck—which is why they had asked me to consider becoming the pastor of their church in the back streets of Liverpool.

I had been thinking and praying about planting a church, but this was not my plan. It was God's plan though, and now I'm so very grateful—not only because God has done amazing things over the years but because he has used this wonderful experience to show me what it means to serve God where you are and how you can, today.

SERVE IN THE NOW

I've played football for most of my life, and I love it, but every time I kick a ball now, I find myself wishing I was in my twenties again because my body can't cash the cheques my mind has written. I wish I could move like I used to, run like I used to, last a whole game like I used to. I can find myself becoming discouraged and downhearted, and not wanting to play anymore.

All of us, once we hit about 35, can be tempted to reminisce about the good old days—when it comes to the Christian life as much as when it comes to our (relative) sporting prowess. We can remember times when we were younger, healthier and less tired, with more money and more energy. Times when, we feel, we were more use or had more capacity, or just were less busy. It was easier to serve then—now, not so much. We start to conclude that there's nothing much we can contribute, and so we don't. In doing so, we miss the opportunities we have to serve in the present—which is why the Bible warns us against this kind of attitude: "Say not, 'Why were the former days better than these?' For it is not from wisdom that you ask this" (Ecclesiastes 7:10).

One of the challenges of being involved in our church replant was that the original church had a heart to see new life in the church community, but how they thought that should look was often rooted in the past, in "the good old days". This was not a bad thing in one sense because they were recalling times of great joy and fruit through the church's ministry. But the challenge is that renewal can't happen by returning to the old ways of serving. Being in your seventies and trying to serve like you did in your thirties, or run things as they were run when you were in your thirties, is not going to work.

In our church replanting journey, we needed to work hard to help people see the reality of what was achievable for us as a church and as individuals, in terms of life stage, capacity and community *in the present*. We needed to stop looking back so that we could work out how we were going to serve well in the present.

THE PROBLEM WITH WHAT'S NEXT

Many of us, though, are mainly not looking back but forwards. We are stuck on our culture's conveyor belt of only ever asking what's next? We move from year to year and life stage to life stage only looking to the next move, job or opportunity. And as we do, there's the temptation to become anxious about what could be next or, conversely, to assume that what comes next will be better than where we are now. At the end of school, we look forward and think, "When I get to college, life will be better". And when we get close to finishing college, we think, "When I get a job and start earning money, things will be better". Then it could be owning a home, or marriage, or having children, or getting promoted, and on and on. We always need (we think) to just get to what's next, and then we can stop chasing and have time and space to take on all the parts of the Christian life that we're quietly putting off.

So when it comes to our Christian service, living only for what's next will negatively impact what we do for the Lord today, just as wishing we were back in the good old days will. "Yesterday" and "tomorrow" are not the moment the Lord calls us to serve in. The age and stage we are in *today* is the age and stage that God wants us to serve in. He doesn't want us to worry about or yearn for what's next, apart from the coming of Jesus. He wants us to serve him from exactly where he has us at this present moment.

If you are in your twenties, serve with the energy and vibrancy of youth because this is what your church needs. If you are in your eighties, you don't need to try to pretend to be 35 again—the church needs your experience and wisdom, which has come from walking many miles of joy and sorrow in service to Jesus.

In Paul's letter to Titus, we see what this can look like...

OLDER BROTHERS AND SISTERS

> *"Older men are to be sober-minded, dignified, self-controlled, sound in faith, in love, and in steadfastness.*

Older women likewise are to be reverent in behaviour, not slanderers or slaves to much wine. They are to teach what is good, and so train the young women to love their husbands and children." (Titus 2:2-4)

When Paul wrote to Titus in Crete, exhorting him to "teach what accords with sound doctrine" (v 1), it was in contrast to the empty talkers and deceivers who were infiltrating the church and upsetting families (1:10-11). In the midst of a culture that was experiencing the distraction and nonsense of damaging voices, Paul encouraged the older generation to serve the younger believers, showing them how to make sense of what it looks like to live in light of the gospel.

This is vital for us today. The voices of deception are loud, and the godless philosophies trying to make sense of life and of our purpose are bombarding us each day. The effect on the younger generation in our churches is weighty, especially when it comes to how they live and serve.

If you are reading this and you are in the twilight years of life, I want to encourage you to recognise that the younger generations in your church need you to serve the body with all the experience that your life has given you. I want to encourage you to see that speaking to the younger generation, sharing your wisdom with them, praying for them every day, and working alongside and cheering them on is as important as anything else you may do in service to Jesus.

Every other week at Cornerstone, some of the older men meet to pray for all the younger men of the church. They sometimes meet for breakfast with the younger guys or go on walks together to listen to and counsel them. Many of these older men have never taught the Bible in a formal setting and have never preached or served as elders or deacons, but they have loved Jesus for decades. They've served God's people in numerous ways and have trusted the Lord through the brokenness of life for many years—and this is all the qualification they need to generously and effectively serve the younger guys.

This particular ministry was put in place because we saw the need. With the women, it was already happening in everyday life. There are some wonderful older women in our church who nurture the faith of younger women and give the kind of gospel perspective on life that only comes from years of experience.

One of the women who does this is Beryl. Beryl is in her seventies and has been part of the church since she was eleven years old. For over 25 years, she led a Bible-study group for the women of our city and over that time thousands (and I mean thousands) of women have sat under her leadership and Bible teaching and are now serving in ministries and churches all over the world. She used the teaching gift God had given her, and God has used it to do great things.

Beryl is a wife, a mother and now a grandmother, living through all the blessings and challenges which that brings. She has also had many health issues. When she came to step down and hand over the teaching role in the Bible study, she told me, "I want to give my life to praying for and encouraging the younger women of our church". And that is what Beryl does—not just for the women, actually, but for everyone. She is a prayer warrior, and when she says she is praying for you, she really is praying for you! She sends dozens of encouraging texts to people every day. She is all about using what she can, today, to see others flourish for the glory of Jesus. Beryl can't and doesn't serve in the ways she used to, but she's not looking back to the "good old days"—she has embraced where God has her and serves the church with a joy that only comes from a life of walking with Jesus. And so these are good days too.

If you are older, you have a treasure chest of wisdom and experience, and you can use all that to serve others.

YOUNGER BROTHERS AND SISTERS

Paul writes to Titus, a young church leader, "Let no one disregard you" (Titus 2:15) as he tells him to "set right what was left undone" (1:5, CSB). He writes something similar to another young leader, Timothy: "Let no one despise you for your youth, but set the believers an example in speech, in conduct, in love, in faith, in purity" (1 Timothy 4:12). This comes after Paul has told him to train for godliness, and to have nothing to do with irrelevant myths but instead to teach the truth. That's a weighty call for such a young leader, and Paul urges him not to let negative comments about his youthfulness block him from serving in this way.

If you are young, give your life now to serving God and his church. Don't get caught up in the noise and nonsense that the evil one would love to distract you with. You have energy, you have passion, you have time, and you have gifts that God has given you. Don't fall into the trap of waiting for what's next and miss the moment to pour yourself out in service for Jesus where he has you now. Glean from the wisdom of the older people in your church and serve.

I'm so thankful that I was in involved in a church replant. I have had the privilege of seeing older saints who thought that their days of serving had ended now serving in ways that they could never have imagined, and I've seen the vibrancy of youthful service being fostered and celebrated as the younger generation give it a go, to the cheers of older brothers and sisters.

So now would be a good moment to pause and reflect on these questions:

- What does it look like for you to serve God from the life stage that you find yourself in?

- Are you spending more time thinking "What next?" rather than how you can serve *now*? What could service look like in your present?

- Do you wish you were young again? Your church

needs you to be the age you are. What would it look like for you to walk with the younger generation in a Titus 2 way? Maybe ask some others of a similar age or life stage and pray about how you can serve in this way together.

SERVE AS YOU CAN

Part of trying to figure out how best to serve is understanding the capacity God has given you. We all have different-sized "capacity plates", and those plates will get bigger or smaller depending on stages and seasons of life.

Remember the parable of the talents and what the king said to the first servant he spoke to once he had heard of the business which that servant had done on the king's behalf:

> "Well done, good servant! Because you have been faithful in a very little, you shall have authority over ten cities." (Luke 19:17)

That servant was faithful with what he had been given, so the king gave him a big reward and increased his capacity to take charge of the ten cities. I'm not suggesting that the more faithful you are, the more capacity God will give you, but I am saying that we should seek to be faithful with the capacity he has given us.

I've always seen myself as a high-capacity person—my days and weeks are pretty full. I like to get involved in things. But high capacity doesn't mean limitless capacity. As I look back over the years, my capacity plate has varied in size in the ebb and flow of different seasons and for different reasons.

I recall sitting at the hospital bed of my eldest daughter, Ella, a number of years ago. She had just had unexpected major surgery after finding out that she had a tumour on her spinal cord, and we had received this news the day after Siân was due to give birth to our fourth child. Our lives were turned upside down. I went from having a relatively large capacity plate to sitting at my daughter's hospital bed on my own, not able to do anything for her, not able to support my wife with our new child or the other kids, and not able to lead the church just as it was about to launch its first plant. Overnight my capacity was reduced—God took the plate that I had been filling and gave me a much smaller one. Despite the initial wrestle in my heart, by his grace I figured out what it looked like to live with a new, smaller plate in that moment. It meant loving and serving my family, and receiving loving service from God's people.

Seasons like this, when illness strikes or trials come, are moments when others can step in and serve us. This is when we rely on other members of the body to bear our burdens, as Paul says in Galatians 6:2, displaying the love of God. Just as we are called to serve, we are also called to allow others to serve us. To not receive this gift of others' service when we are in need of it is to deceive ourselves into thinking we have everything in hand or are capable of carrying it all when clearly we aren't (v 3).

We are called to serve as we can—not as we can't. So work out what you can do in the moment you're in and step up to serve sacrificially. But do it in a way that, while it's stretching, is sustainable. Accept that, at times, this will probably mean receiving the gift of having others limp along with you as they help you carry your burdens. Just as we need to avoid feeling proud or resentful when we think that we're doing more than someone else (because, after all, we don't know the loads they're carrying), we don't need to feel crushed that we're doing less. If you're doing what you can, in the Lord's strength, according to your own capacity, that's pleasing to the Lord.

Again, it's about not being so focused on what you can't do that you forget to do what you can. I was taught this a number of years ago when some of us from church started playing five-a-side soccer weekly with non-believing friends and neighbours. The hope was to build relationships, share the gospel and see them come to know Jesus. One of the guys who started playing with us was called Marco. Marco owned and managed a curry house not far from the church, and it very quickly became our church's go-to place for Indian food. After one of our games, a few of us were going for a drink, and naturally we invited Marco. "Sorry, I can't," said Marco. "I've got to get back to the restaurant for John."

"What do you mean, 'Get back for John'?" I said.

"John comes and works in the restaurant so I can play football with you guys."

"John works in your restaurant? Every week? For free?" I said, shocked.

"Yes—every week, for free. I want to pay him, but he won't take it."

John was one of the elders in our church. He wasn't able to kick a ball around with us, but he really wanted Marco to know Jesus, and so, it turned out, for months he had quietly worked in Marco's restaurant, for free, so that Marco could play football and be among Christians. I'm so moved by this kind of service for Jesus. There is a man who understood his ability and capacity and then used it to serve his Saviour.

God has given us different-sized capacity plates, but we all sit at the same table. Our combined service enables us to serve effectively where God has us and invite others to join us at the table.

SERVE WHERE YOU ARE

"To each is given the manifestation of the Spirit for the common good ... For just as the body is one and has many members, and all the members of the body, though many, are one body, so it is with Christ. For in one Spirit we were all baptized into one body..."

(1 Corinthians 12:7, 12-13)

1 Corinthians 12 is, as we've seen, one of the great "gifts passages" of the New Testament. But in it, Paul spends a lot of time linking the area of gifts to the image of a body. He wants to show that gifts are not given for self-indulgence but for building up the church and its mission. Gifts should always be considered within the context of a co-operating community. God has given you as a gift to the church you are part of, and with that he has also given you gifts to serve his people in your church family for their good. God wants you to serve him in and through your service to his people in your church.

The church universal is the body of Christ, so as we serve our local church, we are serving the wider church. Some may serve regularly through networks or denominations and other ministries, and some may use their gifts and capacity to serve regularly in their local community, but both are always best done while being rooted in a local community of believers. Being led by godly leaders and surrounded by godly people who will help, encourage, disciple and serve with different gifts to yours is what it means to experience gifts being used for the common good.

As it happens, I'm writing this chapter in the lobby of a hotel because I'm away from my family and church family for a few days in order to help serve brothers and sisters who belong to other churches from across the country. This is a privilege, and I love it. But I suspect that other people look at this aspect of my ministry and think, "Oh, that must be so much fun and so exciting—to get to serve in that way". But service in this capacity does not replace or come close to the joy and life-giving benefit I experience from serving with and within my church family and, as part of that, my local community. That shouldn't be surprising because our church is the place in which God has put each of us to serve, and so this is where our service should be rooted. Of course you may have opportunities to serve elsewhere too, and that's great—but they shouldn't come at the expense of serving within your body—your church family.

SERVE IN GOD'S STRENGTH

God does not ask us to do what he does not equip us to do. And he does not ask us to go where he will not go with us.

The prophet Jeremiah was afraid to speak the word of God to Israel because he felt he was too young. God told him not to be afraid and that he would be with him and would deliver him (Jeremiah 1:4-8).

Standing before the risen Jesus, the small group of disciples—some worshipping and some doubting—were told to go and make more disciples, turning the world upside down. And Jesus promised to be with them (Matthew 28:16-20).

The apostle Paul worked hard in serving and ministering to churches in order to see people mature in Christ. (There was a guy with a *huge* capacity plate!) But he knew that the energy that he had was supplied by the God who was with him and working powerfully in and through him (Colossians 1:28-29).

The promise that God would be with Jeremiah and the disciples is for us too. The strength he gave Paul and so many others in the Bible is for us too, as we serve him with our lives. God doesn't ask us to serve him and then leave us to do it on our own—he is right with us. He does not ask for anything from us that he has not already given us—the love, ability, gifts and energy to serve him in ways that truly please him.

We serve because he has served us. We serve out of love for the Lord Jesus. We serve as humble, joyful living sacrifices, with what he's given us, in the way we can, today. And as we do, we can know that he is smiling on us, that he is using our labours to build up our church and impact our community, and that he is looking forward to the day when he greets us with "Well done, good and faithful servant".

ACTION STEPS

- Is your service rooted in your local church?

- Read through Romans 12 and 1 Corinthians 12, spotting the implications for you and your church, and pray through what service looks like for you in your context.

ACKNOWLEDGEMENTS

What a privilege and blessing it's been to spend time thinking through how we can best serve God and his people. I want to first thank Acts 29 and The Good Book Company for asking me to do this. It came as a big surprise but has proved to be a wonderful privilege and has blessed my heart greatly—thank you!

To the amazing team at The Good Book Company, especially Carl Laferton, a big thank-you. Carl, your patience, guidance, insight and editing skill have been stretched with me, brother, and I'm grateful for you and your encouragement. You and your team are a gift to the church.

Thank you, Cornerstone Church Liverpool and Cornerstone Collective churches. Over the past 15 years, we have grown from a small church replant to a vibrant congregation and a communion of churches committed to serving together for the name of Jesus. You have been and are one of the greatest joys of my life—I love you, family.

To the elders and staff of Cornerstone Church Liverpool, I could not have asked for a better team of people to serve Jesus' precious church with. Thank you for encouraging me, for being patient with me and for loving me and my family so well.

Mum and Dad, you have served Jesus in ways that have impacted my life and the lives of Neil, Carl, Debbie and David (and many others) like no one else. Thank you for your Christ-like example of how to serve God and his people through times of suffering and times of blessing.

My dear Siân, after the Lord Jesus you are the greatest gift I have ever been given, and serving alongside you since we were 17 has been the greatest joy. Our partnership in the gospel is evidence of his wonderful grace, and I pray for many more years of serving him together. Thank you for being my biggest encourager during this project and in life. I love you, honey.

And finally, to my Lord and Saviour, Jesus Christ, thank you for saving me and giving me the privilege of serving you and your people. I love you, Lord.

All the glory to him!

DISCUSSION GUIDE FOR SMALL GROUPS

1. WHO DO WE SERVE?

1. "God's command to let his people go [in Exodus 8:1] was for the purpose of serving him" (p 16). Is that how you usually think of life as one of God's people?

2. *Read 1 Peter 2:9-10.* What do these verses remind us about who we are as a church? How should this shape how we relate to God and to each other?

3. "Before you figure out what it means to serve ... you need to know exactly who it is you are serving. You need to know who you are and what your purpose is" (p 24-25). How would you sum up who you are serving, who you are, and what your purpose is, based on what you have read?

4. *Read John 13:3-17, 34-35.* How does Jesus' example here shape our view of what it means to serve one another? What most challenges or inspires you here?

5. Our call is to serve God, his church and his world. Which of those do you think you most focus on as a church and individually? (Think about preaching, prayers, giving and time.) Is there one which might be at risk of being de-emphasised?

2. WHY DO WE SERVE?

1. How do you respond to the idea that "loving the people" isn't enough to keep us serving?

2. *Read Mark 10:35-45.* What would James and John's "why" have been when it came to serving others? What other misguided "whys" do you think are common?

3. Can you think of a time when you've wondered, "Why am I doing this?" What circumstances make it difficult to serve?

4. *Read Romans 12:1-2 and Philippians 2:3-7.* What does a Jesus-like humility look like for us today? Do you think you can grow in that mindset?

5. What do you think your attitude tends to be towards serving as part of your church? Has this chapter reinforced or reshaped that attitude in any way?

3. GOOD AND FAITHFUL SERVANT

1. Can you think of times when service has been a real joy to you? How much of the time does it feel that way?

2. *Read Romans 12:3.* "Remember that you are not the golden child in the kingdom of God and your church— God is not lucky to have you on his team, and you have not earned anything that you have. But, at the same time, remember that you are God's child, even when you feel that everything around you is saying the opposite" (p 44). Can you think of times when you've forgotten one or other of these truths? What goes wrong in our serving when we make one mistake or the other?

3. The chapter lists four aspects of Jesus' service: love, humility, suffering and joy. Which of these aspects do you find most striking? Can you think of an example of what each of these things might look like for us today?

4. Read through the thoughts Steve lists on page 52. Do you recognise any of them as something you're tempted to feel? What truth about Jesus would help you defeat that?

5. How can you encourage each other to think more about Jesus' love than your service? How will you remind each other that God loves to say, "Well done" when we serve out of love for him and for others?

4. SERVE AS THE PERSON GOD HAS MADE YOU TO BE

1. "How has, and how is, God shaping and preparing me for service to him and the church?" (page 62). How would you answer this question yourself?

2. In what ways do you tend to define "what you bring to the table", either positively or negatively? What impact does this have on how you see yourself and your part in your church?

3. "The only living sacrifice I can give is my life, not someone else's. My life, with all its imperfections, weaknesses, experiences, moments and gifts. What you bring to the table of the kingdom is you!" (page 58). Do you need to be liberated, encouraged, or humbled by this?

4. *Read 2 Corinthians 12:9-10.* What do you think it means that God's "power is made perfect in weakness"? Perhaps you can think of some examples of people who have felt weak (whether because of physical limitations, past experiences or something else) yet have served God—how do their lives illustrate this passage?

5. How can you foster a culture in your church where weakness is not seen as something to be resented and a barrier to service, but instead as a way to serve in God's strength and for his glory?

5. SERVE WITH WHAT GOD HAS GIVEN YOU

1. *Read Romans 12:4-6.* Why is this an exciting vision of a church?

2. How do you think your church is doing in terms of people's willingness to serve? Are there ways in which too little is expected, or too much is demanded? What could you do to foster a healthy sense of being one body in Christ?

3. Reading the list of gifts that God gives his people on pages 70-72, which are the ones your church is great at encouraging, fostering and celebrating? Are there any that you think might be underemphasised or undervalued? What could you do about this?

4. Spend some time in self-examination (see page 80) and thinking about your experience (page 80-81), and share your thoughts together.

5. In pairs or threes (aiming to be in a group with people who know you fairly well), ask each other the questions on page 82.

6. Think about this book as a whole and what you have taken from it. What are some encouraging truths that you want to remember? What are some concrete changes you want to make (or pray about) in your life?

6. SERVE WHERE GOD HAS PLACED YOU

1. How does the "problem of what's next" tend to present itself in your lives or in your church?

2. *Read Titus 2:2-4.* How have you seen these lived out, or how have you benefitted personally from these kinds of relationships?

3. What does it mean to "serve in God's strength"? What do you think you might do more of, or do differently, if you consciously rely on God's strength and not your own?

4. Share two or three encouragements about who Jesus is and who we are as his people that you are going to take from this book.

5. Share two or three concrete changes you want to make (or pray about) as a result of reading this book.

RESOURCES FOR SMALL GROUPS

Access the free small-group kit at loveyourchurchseries.com. The free kit includes a video introduction to each session as well as downloadable PDFs of a discussion guide and worksheets. Each session is based on a chapter of the book.

loveyourchurchseries.com

LOVE YOUR CHURCH

thegoodbook.com
thegoodbook.co.uk